MAPPING EARTHFORMS

Oceans and Seas

REVISED AND UPDATED

Catherine Chambers
and Nicholas Lapthorn

Heinemann Library
Chicago, Illinois

Customer Service 888-454-2279
Visit our Web site at www.heinemannraintree.com

Designed by Richard Parker and Q2A solutions
Illustrations: Jeff Edwards
Picture Research: Hannah Taylor
Production: Duncan Gilbert

Originated by Chroma Graphics (Overseas) Pte. Ltd
Printed and Bound in China by Leo Paper Group

11 10 09 08 07
10 9 8 7 6 5 4 3 2 1

New edition ISBNs: 978-1-4034-9603-4 (hardcover)
                   978-1-4034-9613-3 (paperback)

Library of Congress Cataloging-in-Publication Data

Chambers, Catherine, 1954-
  Oceans and seas / Catherine Chambers and Nicholas Lapthorn. -- 2nd ed.
    p. cm. -- (Mapping earthforms)
  Includes bibliographical references and index.
  ISBN-13: 978-1-4034-9603-4 (library binding - hardcover)
  ISBN-10: 1-4034-9603-X (library binding - hardcover)
  ISBN-13: 978-1-4034-9613-3 (pbk.)
  ISBN-10: 1-4034-9613-7 (pbk.)
  1. Ocean--Juvenile literature. 2. Seas--Juvenile literature. [1. Ocean. 2. Seas.] I. Lapthorn, Nicholas. II. Title.

  GC21.5.C43 2007
  508.3162--dc22
                            2006037719

Acknowledgments
The publishers would like to thank the following for permission to reproduce photographs:
Aspect Picture Library p. **5** (Derek Bayes); Bryan & Cherry Alexander Photography pp. **22**, **23**; Corbis/Dallas Morning News p. **25** (Barbara Davidson); Ecoscene pp. **20** (C Cooper), **27** (P Fernby); Getty Images/Riser p. **4**; Oxford Scientific pp. **7** (C Bromhall), **24** (K Westerskov); Photolibrary pp. **16** (Pacific Stock), **19** (Konrad Wothe); Photolibrary.com (Australia) p. **9**; Science Photo Library p. **15** (Alexis Rosenfeld); Seapics.com p. **18** (Bob Cranston); Still Pictures pp. **13** (Don Hinrichson), **21** (Fred Dott), **10** (Klaus Andrews), **26** (Paul Glendell).

Cover photograph reproduced with permission of Corbis/zefa/Gary Bell

Contents

Any words appearing in the text in bold, **like this**, are explained in the Glossary. You can find the answers to Map Active questions on page 29.

What Are Oceans and Seas?

When you see a photograph of Earth taken from space, you will see mostly blue. This blue is the world's oceans and seas. They are huge bodies of salt water that cover nearly 71 percent of Earth's surface. The edges of oceans can be marked by the coasts of huge land masses called **continents**, by underwater ridges of rock, and by surges of flowing water called **currents**.

Seas are generally smaller than oceans and are mostly surrounded by land. Some seas run between two strips of land and open out into oceans. Others are found as large inlets in the coastline.

◀ The ocean is incredibly powerful and can affect our lives in many ways. The ocean is also extremely deep in places, and a lot of it is still unexplored.

How have oceans and seas formed?

Oceans and seas formed millions of years ago. Great splits in Earth's **crust** separated the continents and left huge **basins**. These filled with water from rivers and streams that ran down from the mountains and hillsides. As the rivers ran, they picked up salts and other chemicals from the rocks. The salts and chemicals were carried all the way to the sea, making it salty.

▼ The oceans and seas have given us a rich supply of food. Shellfish can be found among rocks and rock pools, such as here in Brittany in northern France.

What do oceans and seas look like?

Oceans and seas have many different depths and colors. Their waves can lap the shores gently or rise to huge peaks that crash onto the coastline.

Supporting life

Oceans and seas are home to a wide range of plant and animal **species**. Humans have lived on coastal shores for many thousands of years, eating the fish, **mammals**, and plants that live in the waters. Over the years, however, we have also **polluted** the waters and threatened ocean life. So what does the future hold for the oceans and seas of the world?

Oceans and Seas of the World

Counting the oceans

There are three major oceans on Earth. These are the Atlantic, Pacific, and Indian Oceans. Toward the **South Pole**, these oceans merge together in a **current** of water called the West Wind Drift. This is near Antarctica, and some scientists call it the Antarctic Ocean or the Southern Ocean.

Near the **North Pole**, the Atlantic reaches a circular stretch of water that many scientists call the Arctic Ocean. Some believe, however, that it is just part of the Atlantic Ocean. The Atlantic and the Pacific Oceans are very large. They have each been divided into two areas—north and south.

▼ This map shows the world's great oceans, and some of the seas, gulfs, channels, and straits that link them together. All of the oceans and seas mentioned in this book are marked on this map.

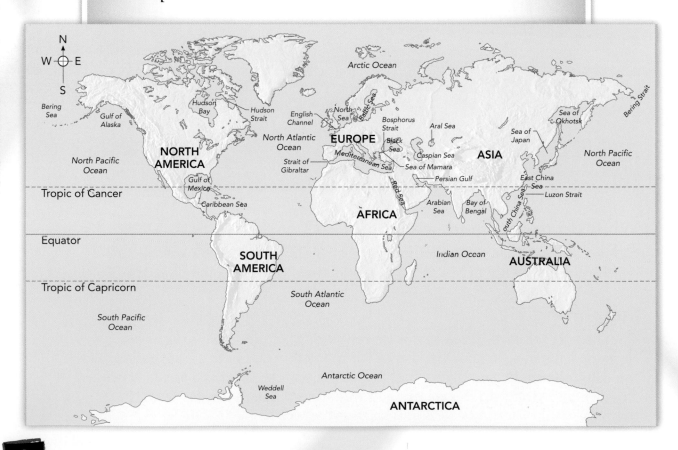

▲ Sometimes one sea leads into another. This is the Sea of Marmara in Turkey. It is connected to the Black Sea by the Bosphorus Strait.

Sorting out the seas

Almost all the seas of the world are connected together in some way. Only a few are cut off, such as the Caspian Sea in Asia. Seas like this are called inland seas, and they are a lot smaller than the other oceans and seas of the world.

Some oceans and seas of the world are connected by channels or **straits**. For example, the Strait of Gibraltar connects the Mediterranean Sea to the Atlantic Ocean. The large oceans merge into each other to form a huge body of seawater that covers much of Earth's surface. Some smaller seas are called gulfs, and these are usually surrounded on two or three sides by land.

How Oceans and Seas Formed

Earth was once a ball of hot gases. Around 4.6 billion years ago, the gases started to cool and form land. **Water vapor** rose into the **atmosphere** to form clouds and rain, which fell back onto the land. Earth's **gravity** caused the rain to flow downhill in streams and rivers. The rivers gathered into a huge **basin**, which became a huge ocean of acid. Over millions of years the waters became less acidic and more salty, similar to today's sea. By about 250 million years ago, the land had formed one huge supercontinent called Pangea. **Continents** were not separate the way they are today.

Around 200 million years ago, the great **plates** of rock that made up Pangea started to break up. They were pushed apart by the movement of hot **magma** under Earth's **crust**. The land split up, and different oceans and **currents** began to flow around the world.

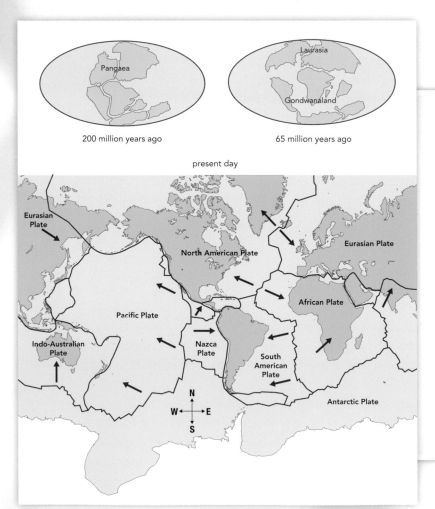

Laurasia

Pangaea

Gondwanaland

200 million years ago   65 million years ago

present day

Eurasian Plate

North American Plate

Eurasian Plate

African Plate

Pacific Plate

Indo-Australian Plate

Nazca Plate

South American Plate

Antarctic Plate

N W E S

◀ As Pangea started to break up, two new continents called Laurasia and Gondwanaland were formed. Gradually they began to break up into the continents that exist today. These sit on top of huge plates that cover Earth's crust. These plates are still moving very slowly.

▼ When waves wash against the shore, they can gradually wear away the rocks around the coast. Sometimes a column of rock called a stack is left on its own. These stacks are called the Twelve Apostles and are found on the coast of Victoria, Australia. The stack in the foreground wore away entirely and collapsed in July 2005.

Moving waters

Very salty or cold waters sink, which causes the surrounding water to move. These huge movements of water are called underwater currents. Winds blow over Earth for long periods of time in one direction. These are called **prevailing winds**. The **rotation** of Earth and the prevailing winds can form currents on the surface of the ocean, such as the Gulf Stream and the Kuro Siwo in the North Pacific (see the map on page 12). Both of these currents are warm, and they make the land near them warmer.

Warm and cold currents around the world affect the **climate** of the continents and help move heat around the world. In addition, moving currents in the ocean can bring water full of **minerals** and **nutrients** from the deep right up to the surface. These waters help sea plants thrive and provide plenty of food for fish.

Tides are caused by the gravity of the Moon and the Sun. As the Moon circles around Earth, its gravity pulls the sea in the same direction. This is sometimes in the opposite direction from the Sun's gravity, and sometimes in the same direction.

Looking Below the Surface

The ocean basin

The ocean **basins** that separate the **continents** are various depths. They get deeper in steps as they get further from the continents. The first step is called the **continental shelf**. This is the shallowest part of the seas and is up to 660 feet (200 meters) deep. It runs out from the shorelines of continents until the sea floor drops down deeper. In some places there is hardly any shelf at all. The waters plunge almost straight down from the continents to a great depth. In other places, the continental shelf stretches out up to 930 miles (1,500 kilometers).

▼ Scientists travel across deep oceans to conduct research. This ship, *Polastern*, is in the Arctic to investigate global warming and climate change.

The second step is called the **continental slope**, which goes down about 8,200 feet (2,500 meters). The third part of the ocean, going even deeper, is the **continental rise**. This is a slope of thick **sediment** that is made up of rock, soil, **minerals**, and the remains of dead plants and animals.

The fourth part of the ocean is a very deep area made up of flat plains and undersea mountains. The deepest place in the oceans is the Mariana Trench in the Pacific, which plunges 6.8 miles (11 kilometers) deep. Most undersea mountains lie in chains and form ridges running along the ocean floor. The Mid-Atlantic Ridge is a chain of undersea mountains and volcanoes. It has been formed as the African and Eurasian Plates pull away from the North American and South American Plates. In some places, such as Iceland and the Azores, these mountains have actually broken through the surface of the sea to form land.

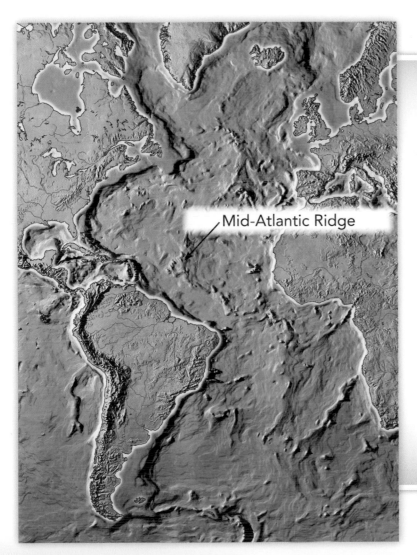

Mid-Atlantic Ridge

◀ Mountain ranges under the ocean are formed when hot, runny **magma** oozes up through cracks in Earth's **crust**, such as where two plates meet. As the magma cools, it forms new ocean crust and pushes the old aside. Over millions of years the old crust forms ridges of mountains on the sea floor. On this map, you can see the Mid-Atlantic Ridge.

The Importance of Seawater

Oceans and seas have many **minerals** dissolved in their waters. They also have gases such as oxygen in them. These are important for plant and animal life. Oceans and seas also help control our **climate**. The Sun's heat **evaporates** moisture from the surface of the water. This travels in the air as **water vapor**. A lot of the water vapor **condenses** to form clouds, which get blown onto the land. The clouds protect Earth from the heat of the Sun. They also bring precious rain.

Much of this rain falls on high ground, where it gathers in streams and rivers. These flow down to the sea, picking up more minerals from the rocks on the way. This movement of water is known as the water cycle, or the **hydrological cycle**. The waters of the oceans and seas also absorb some harmful gases from the air. This helps reduce the problem of **global warming**.

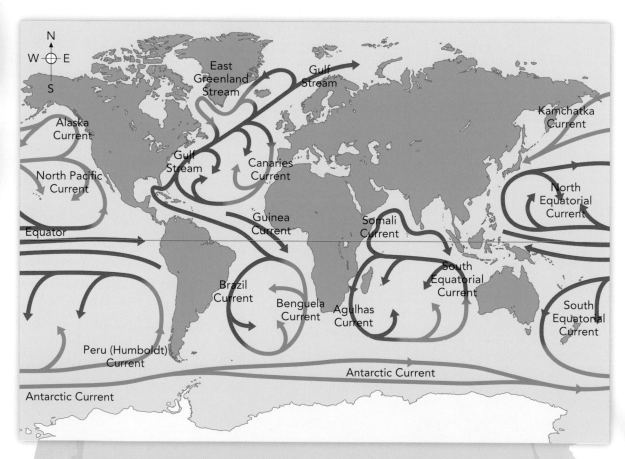

MAP ACTIVE

Look at the currents on the map. How are the temperatures of most currents linked to their locations in the world?

▲ You can sometimes tell the different depths of ocean waters by their color. Here, along the Great Barrier Reef off the east coast of Australia, the shallow parts near the shore of the island are a lighter color than the deeper parts.

What is seawater like?

There is a lot of salt in the oceans and seas. Some seas, such as the Red Sea, have very high levels. Seawater also contains elements such as magnesium, calcium, and potassium. The temperature of seawater varies around the world from 86 °F (28 °C) in **tropical** areas to 29 °F (-1.4 °C) in the **polar regions**. The water temperature in polar regions is just above the freezing temperature of seawater. This is different from freshwater, which freezes at 32 °F (0 °C). However warm or cold it is, seawater temperature does not change much throughout the day.

The Mighty Pacific

The Pacific is the oldest, largest, and deepest of our oceans. Some of the rocks on its seabed were formed at least 200 million years ago. The ocean contains around 50 percent of Earth's free-moving water (not including ice, which is solid water). The Pacific also holds the record for the deepest point in the world, which is about 6.8 miles (11 kilometers) below the surface. This point lies in the Mariana Trench, east of the Philippine Islands.

The Pacific Ocean's northern boundary is the Bering Strait. Its southern boundary is Antarctica. To the east, the ocean meets the west coasts of North and South America. To the west, the ocean meets Asia, the islands of Malaysia and Indonesia, and the **continent** of Australia.

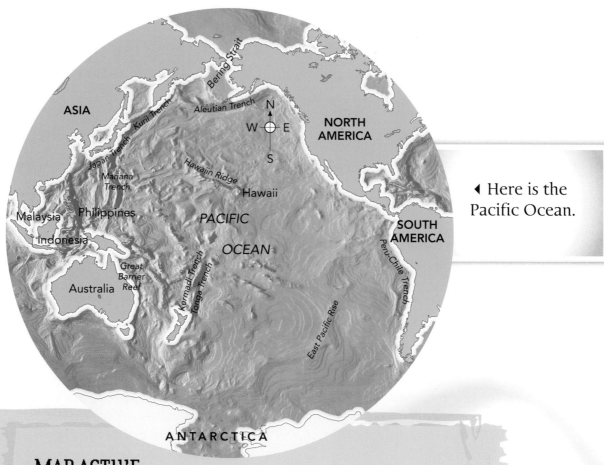

◀ Here is the Pacific Ocean.

MAP ACTIVE

Look at the trenches in the Pacific Ocean and then look at the map on page 8. What do you notice?

▼ Visiting the deepest part of the ocean is a dangerous job. Submersible (underwater) machines such as the *Nautile* can go to depths of 4 miles (6 kilometers). It has been used to study the wreck of the *Titanic* in the Atlantic Ocean.

The **continental shelf** of the Pacific Ocean is narrow along the coasts of North and South America, but wide near Asia and Australia. The ocean floor is split by wide trenches and studded with chains of mountains. Some of these break the ocean surface and form islands.

Scientists believe that there may be more than 30,000 islands rising from the floor of the Pacific Ocean. The South Pacific area has islands made of **coral**. The western Pacific has a long arc of volcanic islands. This forms part of the Pacific Ring of Fire, so named because of all its volcanoes and earthquakes.

Pacific coral reefs, such as the Great Barrier Reef in Australia, are full of amazing sea life. Near South America, the ocean **currents** bring lots of **nutrients**, so there are many fish. Local fishers catch anchovies in large quantities.

Plants of the Oceans and Seas

Plants in the water

Green, leafy plants need sunlight to make food so that they can grow. In the oceans and seas, these types of plant can only grow where the Sun's rays reach down into the water. Most of these plants lie in the **continental shelf** area and in the top part of the **continental slope** of the ocean.

The plants in water are mainly **algae**. Algae range from tiny, microscopic plants to fleshy-leaved seaweed such as giant kelp, which can grow to more than 200 feet (60 meters) tall. The larger algae often have long, thick stalks that are attached to the seabed. Some attach themselves to rocks near the shore using clinging roots. They have a slimy coating to stop them from drying up when the tide is out.

The smaller algae floating in the ocean are also known as phytoplankton. They are eaten by tiny creatures called zooplankton, which in turn are eaten by fish. Without algae there would be very little animal life in the oceans and seas.

Not all sea plants need sunlight to grow, however. In the 1970s scientists found tiny plant **bacteria** growing on rocks very deep down in the ocean. These rocks are near hot **volcanic vents**. The bacteria can grow here without sunlight because the hot vents release a chemical called hydrogen sulphide. This chemical can make the bacteria grow.

◀ Giant kelp grows in thick forests in warm, shallow waters near the coast. These forests provide food and hiding places for many different types of sea animals.

▲ The sea buckthorn bush has lots of tightly packed branches and short, thin leaves. This stops them from being broken off by the wind. The bright orange berries are clustered closely together against the branches for protection. The bush can grow up to 16 feet (5 meters) tall and is found along many parts of Europe's coast.

Plants on the coast

Plants on the coast have to cope with strong winds and salty air. Some survive in **salt marshes** that lie between the land and the sea. Plants that are able to grow in salty conditions are known as halophytes. Many of them get rid of the salt through thousands of tiny holes in their leaves.

Sea Animals

The oceans and seas provide a huge range of **habitats** for animals. These habitats range from the dark, cold depths of the oceans to muddy shores. Like sea plants, most sea animals live in the sunlit area of the **continental shelf** and the upper part of the **continental slope**. Many animals, however, live deeper than this.

Full of fish

Fish breathe through **gills**, which absorb oxygen in seawater into their bodies. Fins help fish move through the water. An air bladder inside the body stops the fish from rolling from side to side. Many fish have a protective layer of **scales**. These are covered with a very thin skin that produces slime. This protects the fish from bumps and scrapes, and stops little **parasites** from attacking the fish.

▼ The Humboldt squid is also known as the red devil. Over the centuries fishers have feared it. It belongs to the mollusk family and catches its prey with its long tentacles. In the middle of its tentacles is a large mouth with a very sharp beak.

Some fish have **adapted** to surviving in the deepest, darkest parts of the ocean. These fish can create their own light. They do this by producing a chemical called phosphorus, which glows. They create light to attract mates, to confuse predators, and to find food.

▲ These bottlenose dolphins are leaping out of the sea. Scientists think they do this to help them hunt for food and to communicate with other dolphins. Many people believe they do it for fun!

Many mollusks

Mollusks are a huge family of animals, with about 100,000 different **species**. Salt-water mollusks range from oysters, which lie still on the ocean floor, to the giant squid. They all have soft bodies, but most are protected by a hard shell.

Sea mammals

Mammals all breathe air, so you might be surprised to find mammals living in the sea. There are many sea mammals, however, and these include seals, sea lions, walruses, whales, dolphins, porpoises, and manatees. They all come up to the surface to breathe air, and many of them can dive to enormous depths for a very long time before needing to take another breath.

Living with the Ocean

The riches of the sea

Fishing has been a way of life for many people for thousands of years. Some of the world's oldest settlements began as small fishing villages on the coast. Fishing provides the world with an important source of food. Some fishers still catch fish using traditional boats, such as canoes. Modern methods, however, allow large numbers of fish to be easily caught by huge fishing ships.

▼ Venice in Italy has been an important trading port for hundreds of years. It is a beautiful city that attracts many tourists. It is made up of a number of marshy islands in a **lagoon**. The port is protected from the ocean by long barriers of sand called sandbars.

Murano

Venice Mainland

Venice

Venice Lido

lagoon entrance

lagoon

sandbar

N
W ⊕ E
S

0   2 miles
0   3 km

People who live near the coast can also farm or collect seaweed. Seaweed can be used as a **fertilizer**. It also supplies **vitamins** and **minerals** humans need. The jelly-like substance in brown **algae** is used to make colors in paints smooth and to give ice cream its creaminess.

Before airplanes and trucks, most of the world's **trade** traveled by sea. Today, trade shipping routes are still very busy, with huge container ships carrying all sorts of goods around the world. These ships dock at large ports where the goods are unloaded and taken away to be sold.

Sea, sun, and sand have attracted millions of people to visit the coast as tourists. This has changed many small fishing villages into huge **resorts**. People have flocked to the coast to find work in hotels and restaurants. For some countries, coastal tourism is the most important industry.

◄ This is an oil platform off the coast of Norway in northern Europe. Oil has brought many people to live by the sea.

Marine minerals

Coastal communities also find work taking minerals from the sea. Salt, magnesium, and bromine are left behind when seawater **evaporates**. Around 17 percent of the world's oil comes from beneath the ocean floor. Sand, gravel, and oyster shells are dug up from the seabed and used in building.

A Way of Life—The Inuit of Canada

The Inuit people have lived on the east coast of Canada for centuries. The different Inuit groups came to North America from the frozen lands of Siberia in Russia more than 4,000 years ago. They have **adapted** their way of life to harsh, snow-covered coastlands in winter, and to short, sunny summers.

The Inuit call the northern part of Canada Nunavut, which means "our land." The area has mountain ranges, forests, and **tundra**. Nunavut includes the sea and the islands along the coast. The sea plays a huge part in the Inuit culture. The coast stretches more than 4,800 miles (7,800 kilometers) and supports fish, sea **mammals**, and seabirds.

◀ An Inuit hunter fishes through a hole in the ice.

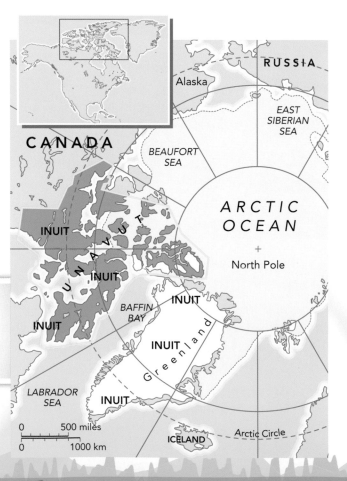

▶ Nunavut is located in Canada.

▲ Many Inuit now use snowmobiles to get around.

Traditional Inuit life

Traditional Inuit use the plants and animals of the coast and sea for their everyday needs. Seals are a good source of food, especially in winter. The Inuit also eat fish, whales, and walruses, which they mostly catch in the summer on the open sea. They cook the fresh meat or preserve it by drying or freezing.

They also make seal skins into warm, waterproof clothes. Winter trousers and boots are made with double layers of skin and fur. The coat is a parka, which is a double-layer pullover with a hood. The skins are also made into **harpoon** lines, and they cover tent frames and boats as well.

Summer homes are made of walrus or seal skins over a whalebone or driftwood frame. The walls of winter houses are made of stones packed with moss and earth. Inuit people burn seal fat to make light and heat.

Today, most Inuit lead more modern lives. Their clothes, food, buildings, and jobs are very different from the traditional ways of living. Many Innuit people live and work in North America's towns and cities.

Sea Changes

The changing climate

Some parts of the world's oceans and seas almost always have stormy waters, such as Cape Horn on the tip of South America. Others have long periods of calm, such as the **doldrums** that lie in parts of the tropics. Mostly, however, the ocean waves change all the time. They change with the tides, the weather, and the seasons of the year.

In recent years some seas have experienced unusually violent seasonal storms. Severe **hurricanes** have battered islands and coastlines. Many scientists believe that these hurricanes are caused by too much sun on the oceans. This **evaporates** more water, which brings heavier rain and stronger winds.

▼ The amount of fish in our oceans is falling. Fishers catch at least 60 million tons of fish every year. On this fish factory ship, thousands of fish are caught, processed, and frozen on board every day. Fish in some areas, such as North Atlantic cod, are in danger of disappearing altogether.

Some scientists think that the **climate** is changing because of increased activity of the Sun. Others think the effects of the Sun are stronger because Earth's protective layer of ozone gases has become thinner. This combines with the greenhouse effect, in which increased carbon dioxide **pollution** in the air traps more heat in the atmosphere. As a result, the climate is changing, and this is affecting oceans and seas across the world.

▲ In September 2005, Hurricane Katrina caused devastating floods in New Orleans. In total, more than 1,500 people were killed in the hurricane and the flooding that followed.

Changing the water

Rivers and streams pour millions of gallons of water into the sea every day. Today, many rivers also carry pollution and waste. Pollution includes chemical **fertilizers** that have soaked into the rivers from farmland and **pesticides** sprayed over huge areas. Raw **sewage** and waste from power stations and factories are sometimes pumped straight into rivers and the sea. This has led to pollution in some seas and has reduced the number of plants and animals living there.

Looking to the Future

The power of the sea

Covering almost 71 percent of Earth's surface, and always moving, the sea is a huge source of energy. If we can capture some of this energy, we will depend less on **fossil fuels**. Fossil fuels cause a lot of **pollution** by releasing gases when we burn them, and when oil spills happen.

Wave and tidal power close to the shore can turn **turbines** that produce electricity. Another idea is to use the ocean's **thermal energy**. This energy comes from the Sun's heat, which has been absorbed by the water. It also comes from ocean **currents**. The heat can be changed into electric energy in a process known as ocean thermal energy conversion.

▼ This bird has been badly affected by an oil spill from a huge oil tanker, the *Sea Empress*. This tanker broke up near Milford Haven in Wales in 1996. The oil killed thousands of birds, fish, and shellfish. It covered the sands and spoiled an area known for its natural beauty and wildlife.

▲ Scientists believe that **global warming** is melting ice in the **polar region**. The **meltwater** is raising the level of seawater. This means that some towns and villages are in danger of being flooded. In some areas **coastal defenses** are being built to protect our coastlines.

Fish forever

The number of fish in the seas is falling. More than 90 percent of the fish caught in the world come from oceans and seas. Many small fish are caught before they can become adults and produce more fish. We can stop catching small fish by using nets with larger meshes. We can also develop more **fish farms** along the coasts, so that fewer fish from the sea need to be caught.

We can also help ocean life by cleaning the waste from our factories and power stations before it flows into the sea. We can increase the amount of freshwater reaching the sea by building fewer **dams** along the rivers. Dams stop water, and the **minerals** in it, from reaching the oceans.

Ocean and Sea Facts

Ten largest seas

These are ten of the largest seas in the world. The column on the right shows their average depths. The table also shows which ocean these seas are connected to.

Sea	Location	Area in square miles (square kilometers)	Average depth in feet (meters)
South China Sea	Pacific	1.4 million (3,685,000)	3,478 (1,060)
Caribbean Sea	Atlantic	1.1 million (2.8 million)	8,448 (2,575)
Mediterranean Sea	Atlantic	971,000 (2.5 million)	4,925 (1,501)
Bering Sea	Pacific	876,000 (2.3 million)	4,892 (1,491)
Gulf of Mexico	Atlantic	596,000 (1.5 million)	5,299 (1,615)
Sea of Okhotsk	Pacific	590,000 (1.5 million)	3,192 (973)
Sea of Japan	Pacific	378,000 (978,000)	5,469 (1,667)
Hudson Bay	Atlantic	316,000 (819,000)	305 (93)
East China Sea	Pacific	290,000 (752,000)	1,148 (350)
North Sea	Atlantic	222,000 (575,000)	308 (94)

Plunging the depths

- The deepest ocean generally is the Pacific, with an average depth of 13,000 feet (4,030 meters). That's more than 2.5 miles (4 kilometers)! It is closely followed by the Indian Ocean, which has an average depth of 12,800 feet (3,900 meters).

- Tsunamis are huge waves caused by undersea earthquakes and volcanic eruptions. One of the most destructive tsunamis happened in December 2004 in the Indian Ocean. A large underwater earthquake off the coast of Indonesia sent a series of huge waves across the Indian Ocean, killing more than 200,000 people as they smashed into coastlines.

- One of the highest waves ever recorded was 90 feet (27 meters) high. It was caused when Hurricane Ivan passed over the Gulf of Mexico in September 2004.

Find Out More

Further reading

Ganeri, Anita. *Earth Files: Oceans.* Chicago: Heinemann Library, 2002.

Hudak, Heather. *Oceans.* New York, NY: Weigl Publishers, Inc., 2005.

Theodorou, Rod. *Amazing Journeys: To the Depths of the Ocean.* Chicago: Heinemann Library, 2006.

Web sites

www.mos.org/oceans/
Find out more about the world's oceans at this exciting site.

www.epa.gov/owow/oceans/kids.html
This Web site from the U.S. Environmental Protection Agency provides information about keeping our oceans clean.

Map Active answers

Page 12: Ocean **currents** that start near the equator and flow away from it are usually warm. This is because the Sun heats the oceans most around the equator. Currents that start near the North and South Poles and flow toward the equator are usually cold.

Page 14: The trenches in the Pacific Ocean are located very close to the boundaries of the Pacific Plate and the Nazca Plate, shown in the map on page 8. This is because trenches often form where two **plates** meet and one starts sliding beneath the other.

Glossary

adapted changed to suit certain conditions

algae simple form of plant life

atmosphere layers of gases that surround Earth

bacteria tiny, one-celled organisms, some of which can cause disease

basin sea or ocean floor that slopes downward like the inside of a sink

climate rainfall, temperature, and wind that normally affect a large area over a long period of time

coastal defense barrier put up to slow and stop flooding in an area next to the sea

condense when gas turns into a liquid as it cools

continent any one of the world's largest continuous land masses

continental rise third step under the ocean that runs from the edge of the continental slope toward the very deep ocean floor

continental shelf relatively shallow area that slopes from the coast of a continent into the ocean

continental slope second step under the ocean that runs from the edge of the continental shelf further into the ocean

coral hard rock made of the skeletons of tiny dead sea animals

crust hard outer layer of Earth

current water that flows constantly in one direction

dam wall that is built across a river valley to hold back water, creating an artificial lake behind it

doldrums region near the equator where there can be long periods of calm weather, making sailing difficult

evaporate turn from solid or liquid into vapor, such as when water becomes water vapor

fertilizer substance added to soil to make plants grow better

fish farm place where fish are bred and raised in large netted areas in the sea

fossil fuel coal, oil, and gas formed from the remains of plants and animals that lived millions of years ago

gill organ on animals living in water that takes in oxygen from the water

global warming gradual (slow) increase in temperature that affects the entire Earth

gravity force that pulls all objects toward Earth

habitat place where a plant or animal usually grows or lives

harpoon spear attached to a line that is often shot from a gun

hurricane wind that blows faster than 75 miles (120 kilometers) per hour

hydrological cycle movement of water between the air, land, and sea

lagoon area of sheltered, shallow water that lies between a coral reef and the shore

magma hot, molten rock that lies below the surface of Earth

mammal animal that feeds its young with its own milk

meltwater water that flows out as ice and snow melt

mineral substance that forms naturally in rock or earth, such as oil or salt

North Pole northernmost tip of the world, in the Arctic region

nutrient substance such as a vitamin or mineral that provides energy needed for growth

parasite animal (or plant) that lives on other animals (or plants) and usually harms them

pesticide chemical that is used to kill plant-eating insects

plate giant piece of Earth's crust that moves slowly over the mantle

polar region area around the North and South Poles

pollute make air, water, or land dirty or impure

prevailing wind wind that mainly blows from one direction

resort place where people stay on vacation

rotation spinning

salt marsh area of low-lying silt and mud around the coast where certain types of salt-tolerant plants can grow

scale small flake of a hard material similar to a finger nail that covers the skin of many types of fish

sediment fine soil and gravel that is carried in water

sewage human waste material

South Pole southernmost tip of the world, in Antarctica

species one of the groups used for classifying animals; animals in the same species are very similar and can mate to produce young

strait narrow strip of water that often connects a sea to an ocean

thermal energy energy from the Sun's heat that can be absorbed by gases, liquids, and solids

trade buying and selling goods

tropical hot and humid area around the middle of Earth

tundra land in the Arctic where the soil is frozen for most of the year, with only the very top layer thawing out in summer

turbine revolving motor that is pushed around by water or steam and can produce electricity

vitamin chemical that bodies need to stay healthy

volcanic vent opening of a volcano that lava, gas, and steam escape from

water vapor water that has been heated so much that it forms a gas that is held in the air

Index